Simple Tips for

Simple Living

for Women

New Leaf Press

First Printing: March 2004

Cover by Left Coast Design, Portland, OR
Interior design by Brent Spurlock
Edited by Jim Fletcher and Roger Howerton

ISBN: 0-89221-574-7
Library of Congress Catalog Card Number: 2003116024

Please visit our web site for more great titles:
www.newleafpress.net

New Leaf Press

A special gift for you

To

EuELYNN KENNEdy Mayo

From

17-)lovember -08

Simple Living

Tip

1

Simplicity is the attempt to see clearly — to know what's important and what matters most. It's taking stock of your life and stripping away the inessential. At the heart of simplicity is the process of self-examination and self-discovery — deciding what you need to be happy. Simplicity is the age-old search for happiness. It is the art of living fully and being fully alive.[1]

The greater part of our happiness or misery depends on our dispositions and not our circumstances.

– Martha Washington

If human beings are perceived as potentials rather than problems, as possessing strengths instead of weaknesses, as unlimited rather that dull and unresponsive, then they thrive and grow to their capabilities.

– Barbara Bush

Simple Living

Tip

2

To freshen the air:

Leave open boxes of baking soda in refrigerators, closets and bathrooms.

Saturate a cotton ball with pure vanilla; place on a saucer in refrigerator or car.

Set out white vinegar in open dishes to destroy odors such as tobacco smoke, fish, or paint.

Set out potpourri in open dishes.

Burn scented candles.

Sprinkle cinnamon on aluminum foil and place it in a hot oven, leaving the door open. As the cinnamon heats, the cinnamon will permeate the house.

Squeeze a few drops of fresh lemon juice into the dust bag of your vacuum cleaner before you start it up.

To deodorize a musty-smelling book, put it in a brown paper bag with baking soda and let sit for approximately one week.

My second favorite household chore is ironing. My first being hitting my head on the top bunk bed until I faint.

– Erma Bombeck

3

Purge, purge, purge! We simply have too much stuff. Possessions take up space, time, money, and emotional energy. And quite often, we are expending these valuable resources on items we haven't used in five years! If an item is beautiful, useful, or loved, keep it. If not, clear the decks. A good rule of thumb is, "If you haven't used it in the last 12 months, you probably won't use it in the next 12."[2]

And he said unto them, Take heed, and beware of covetousness: for a man's life consisteth not in the abundance of the things which he possesseth.
– Luke 12:15

Brethren, I count not myself to have apprehended: but this one thing I do, forgetting those things which are behind, and reaching forth unto those things which are before, I press toward the mark for the prize of the high calling of God in Christ Jesus.
– Philippians 3:13-14

4

MONDAY (Washing)

Lord, help me **wash away** all my selfishness and vanity, so I may serve You with perfect humility through the week ahead.

TUESDAY (Ironing)

Dear Lord, help me **iron out** all the wrinkles of prejudice I have collected through the years so that I may see the beauty in others.

WEDNESDAY (Mending)

Oh God, help me **mend** my ways so I will not set a bad example for others.

THURSDAY (Dusting)

Lord Jesus, help me to **dust** out all the many faults I have been hiding in the secret corners of my heart.

FRIDAY (Shopping)

O God, give me the grace to **shop wisely** so I may purchase eternal happiness for myself and all others in need of love.

SATURDAY (Cooking)

Help me, my Savior, to **brew** a big kettle of brotherly love and serve it with clean, sweet bread of human kindness.

SUNDAY (Resting)

O God, I have prepared my house for you. Please come into my heart as my **honored guest** so I may spend the day and the rest of my life in Your presence.[3]

> *When I stand before God at the end of my life, I would hope that I would not have a single bit of talent left, and could say, "I used everything you gave me."*
>
> – Erma Bombeck

Six days shalt thou labor and do all thy work; But the seventh day is the Sabbath of the LORD thy God . . .
– Exodus 20:9-10

5

Fruit and flowers may be preserved

from decay and fading by immersing

them in a solution of gum Arabic and

water two or three times, waiting

a sufficient time between each

immersion to allow the gum to dry.

This process covers the surface of the

fruit with a thin coat of gum, which

is entirely impervious to the air, thus

preventing the decay of the fruit or

flower. Roses thus preserved have all the beauty of freshly picked ones, though they have been separated from the parent stock many months.[4]

As for man, his days are as grass: as a
flower of the field, so he flourisheth.
– Psalm 103:15 (RSV)

Cheerfulness and contentment are great beautifiers
and are famous preservers of youthful looks.
– Charles Dickens

6

God's Emergency Phone Numbers

When in sorrow - call John 14

When friends fail you - Psalm 27

If you want to be fruitful - John 15

When you have sinned - Psalm 51

When you worry - Matthew 6:19-34

When you are in danger - Psalm 91

When God seems far away - Psalm 139

When your faith needs stirring - Hebrews 11

When you are lonely and fearful - Psalm 23

When you grow bitter and critical - I Cor. 13

Paul's secret to happiness - Col. 3:12-17

Understanding of Christianity - 2 Cor. 5:15-19

When you feel down and out - Romans 8:31

When you want peace and rest - Matthew 11:25-30

When the world seems bigger than God - Psalm 90

When you want Christian assurance - Romans 8:1-30

When you leave home for labor or travel - Psalm 121

When your prayers grow narrow or selfish - Psalm 67

For a great invention/opportunity - Isaiah 55

When you want courage for a task - Joshua 1

How to get along with fellow men - Romans 12

When you think of investment and returns - Mark 10

If you are depressed - Psalm 27

If your pocket book is empty - Psalm 37

If you're losing confidence in people - 1 Cor. 13

If people seem unkind - John 15:18-27

If discouraged about your work - Psalm 126

If you find the world growing small and yourself great
- Psalm 19

Human successes, like human failures, are composed of one action at a time and achieved by one person at a time.

– Patsy H. Sampson

Alternate Phone Numbers

For dealing with fear - Psalm 34:7

For security - Psalm 121:3

For assurance - Mark 8:35

For reassurance - Psalm 145:18 [5]

> *For this very reason make every effort to supplement your faith with virtue, and virtue with knowledge, and knowledge with self-control, and self-control with steadfastness, and steadfastness with godliness, and godliness with brotherly affection, and brotherly affection with love.*
> – 2 Peter 1:5-7 (RSV)

7

Phone cards make a **great, yet simple, gift** when tucked into a card which says "only a phone call away." While few of us need more dust catchers or clothes, and finding that perfect gift seems impossible, we can all use the support of family and friends. The true gift is not really the phone card — it is your willingness to let them know you're ready to listen when they call and enough foresight to make it easy for them no matter what their circumstances might be . . . what better way to let someone know you truly care.

Never record a greeting, on your **telephone answering machine** that tells callers you are not at home or are away for few days. Such messages can unwittingly invite burglars.

Clean your telephone with rubbing alcohol on a cloth, but keep the moisture from getting into the holes in the mouthpiece.

Be connected to your world. Whatever you are doing in this moment, really experience it. Too much of our lives are spent in the "maybes" or "could bes" – so much so that the joys we could experience now are overlooked and lost in the reflections and yearning for the "never weres" in our lives. Living is a verb, a word of action, and not just a period of sleepwalking between dreams and disappointments. Whatever you do, do it, truly experience it, make it a moment that matters to you so when you do look back, you have a treasury of accomplishments savored, and not unhappy regrets for lost time and opportunity.

The bitterest tears shed over graves are for words left unsaid and deeds left undone.

– Harriet Beecher Stowe

Who can find a virtuous woman? For her price is far above rubies. . . . She looketh well to the ways of her household, and eateth not the bread of idleness. Her children arise up, and call her blessed; her husband also, and he praiseth her.

– Proverbs 31:10-28

8

Old tee shirts make great rags for dusting, polishing and general household cleaning.

To ease a **tight zipper**, rub its teeth with candle wax, soap, or petroleum jelly. Wipe off the residue with a tissue.

To sharpen **dull scissors**, use them to cut a piece of sandpaper into strips.

To **remove crayon marks** from wood furniture, rub mayonnaise on them. Let it stand for ten minutes and then rub with a soft cloth.

Never store any flammable items (such as household cleaners, solvents, paint supplies, or old rags) near a gas water heater.

To **prevent the paint smell** when painting inside your home, add a few drops of vanilla extract to the paint when stirring or mixing. This will remove the unpleasant smell but won't affect your color.

Rejoice in the LORD, O ye righteous: for praise is comely for the upright.
– Psalm 33:1

Simple Living

Tip

9

Deal with new paperwork right now. Rather than tossing the mail in a pile, sort incoming paperwork as you receive it. Toss the junk mail, envelopes, and inserts, and group the rest according to what you have to do to it.

Create a system for filing important papers; have individual file folders labeled for separate categories and place them in one central location.[6]

Save time and steps by **wearing a fanny pack** while cleaning. That way, when you find little things — a lost doll shoe, a screw that must have fallen out of something — you can just pick them up and continue on, instead of backtracking for each of them.[7]

Who shall ascend into the hill of the LORD?
or who shall stand in his holy place?
He that hath clean hands, and a pure heart; who hath
not lifted up his soul unto vanity, nor sworn deceitfully.
– Psalm 24:3-4

What a lot we lost when we stopped writing
letters. You can't reread a phone call.

– Liz Carpenter

Stick a button to the **end of a roll of tape**, making the end easy to find. Move the button with every use. Make sure to keep it out of reach of small children who could swallow the button.

To **recycle envelopes**, carefully open the envelope and turn it inside out, so the address is on the inside. Re-glue or tape the flaps down.

Spray the inside of a mayonnaise jar white. Store it in the refrigerator as **a hiding place for money** or valuables.

Use bread or damp cotton wool to pick up the fragments of **broken glass** safely.

Wise men lay up knowledge: but the mouth
of the foolish is near destruction.
– Proverbs 10:14

Life is uncertain. Eat dessert first.

– Ernestine Ulmer

11

For **yucky tasting medicines**, have a child suck an ice cube before giving him the medicine. It will chill the taste buds and he will swallow the medicine easily.

For **minor throat irritation**, mix a teaspoon of table salt with a glass of hot water and gargle three or four times a day.

To ease the pain of **minor burns**, vanilla or a paste of baking soda and water will help to take away the initial pain.

For **burns and scalds**, place a crushed onion on the burn and cover with a bandage.

For relief from a **toothache,** bite a clove.

Use honey to moisturize a **dry throat**.

A merry heart doeth good like a medicine.
– Proverbs 17:22

Laughter is the best form of medicine.
– Eugene Lam

12

Heating and cooling seldom-used rooms in the home may be wasting energy and money. Consider closing the air ducts and doors in rooms used mostly for storage and occasionally for guests. Closing unused rooms may reduce heating and cooling costs by up to 20 percent, depending on the proportion of your home's total square footage the closed rooms comprise. Check with the dealer of the heating and cooling system to determine whether closing off rooms has the potential to harm the system.

And the Lord said, Who then is that faithful and wise steward, whom his lord shall make ruler over his household, to give them their portion of meat in due season?
– Luke 12:42

13

Consolidate your activities. Whether you're running errands, doing paperwork, or cleaning the house, try to do a lot of one thing at a time. Do all of your filing THEN make your phone calls, THEN sit down and write some letters. Avoid hopping back and forth between activities. Also, arrange your trips geographically so that you aren't returning to the same area three times in one day.[8]

Do it now! My mantra. Whenever possible, I do a small task immediately, so I don't have to put it on a list or think about it again. This is huge.[9]

I could not, at any age, be content to take my place by the fireside and simply look on. Life was meant to be lived. Curiosity must be kept alive. One must never, for whatever reason, turn his back on life.

–Eleanor Roosevelt

Learn to say no!! "No" is the most difficult word in the English language. It is not required that you participate in every activity that comes your way. Choose only those that really mean something to you and know your limits. It is better to tell someone "no" than to accept the additional responsibility, become overwhelmed, and do a shoddy job.[10]

The fear of the LORD is the beginning of wisdom: a good understanding have all they that do his commandments: his praise endureth for ever.

– Psalm 111:10

We must learn our limits. We are all something, but none of us are everything.

– Blaise Pascal

Simple Living

Tip

15

Recipe for a Joyful Day

— One relationship with God

— 1/2 cup gratefulness

— A spinkling of songs in your heart

— A heaping spoonful of prayer

— A tablespoon of children's giggles

— A dollop of humor

— A dash of sunshine

— One pair of rose-colored glasses

— Lay out one relationship with God as the base. Add gratefulness, songs, and prayer. Mix thoroughly. Next, fold in giggles, humor, and sunshine. Bake overnight with a good night's sleep. Serve with a cheerful attitude and joyful determination. Feeds the hungry hearts of one to millions.[11]

Remember that happiness is a way of travel — not a destination.

– Roy M. Goodman

16

For **insect bites and stings**, wash the sting with vinegar.

For **indigestion**, drink one teaspoon of mint juice mixed with an equal amount of honey and lemon juice.

To me good health is more than just exercise and diet. It's really a point of view and a mental attitude you have about yourself.

– Angela Lansbury

*Drink no longer water, but use a little wine for thy stomach's
sake and thine often infirmities.*
– 1 Timothy 5:23

Simple Living
Tip

17

To get rid of **lizards and cockroaches**, keep empty eggshell halves at the places where you have spotted them.

Keep roaches away by placing cucumber peelings in drawers and in corners. Replace them when they dry out.

You may have to fight a battle more than once to win it.
– Margaret Thatcher

And every creeping thing that creepeth upon the earth shall be an abomination.

– Leviticus 11:41

18

For a quick **insecticide** for bees or flies, try spraying them with hairspray.

To **get rid of houseflies**, put a sponge in a saucer and saturate with oil of lavender and place it where the flies can easily get to it.

Time's fun when you're having flies.

– Kermit the Frog

And the LORD did according to the word of Moses; and he removed the swarms of flies from Pharaoh, from his servants, and from his people; there remained not one.

– Exodus 8:31

19

As a **substitute for mothballs**, put leftover pieces of bar soap in a vented plastic bag and place the bag with clothes before storing them. Moths will be repelled, and the clothes will smell good when used again.

To **keep ants out of the house**, find where the ants are entering the house and sprinkle cinnamon or ground pepper in their trail.

Some people say you can draw a chalk line and the ants will not cross it. Others say to sprinkle a little bit of baby powder on the trail. Try a remedy and see if it works.

The ants are a people not strong, yet they prepare their meat in the summer.
– Proverbs 30:25

It's not so much how busy you are, but why you are busy. The bee is praised; the mosquito is swatted.

– Marie O'Conner

Simple Living

Tip

20

A great **cure for turmoil, anger, fear, and doubt** is silence. Let this silence be a time of prayer, or self-reflection, or even appreciation for all that God has blessed in your life. Take just a moment for yourself by giving that moment to God. Just stop and listen to what God may be wanting to share with you.

Be still, and know that I am God: I will be exalted among the heathen, I will be exalted in the earth

– Psalm 46:10

Silence is a great peacemaker.

– Henry Wadsworth Longfellow

How to get the last word during an argument — make it an apology.

Lighten your burdens and drop that grudge! It's said that having a spirit of non-forgiveness is like drinking poison — and waiting for the other person to die!

Don't cry over spilled milk, pour yourself another glass.

– Melissa McGee

Let not the sun go down upon your wrath.
– Ephesians 4:26

22

To keep the **cat's litter box** smelling fresh, mix baby powder in with the litter.

To **rid pets of skunk smell**, shampoo with a mixture of one quart 3% hydrogen peroxide, a quarter cup baking soda, and one tablespoon liquid dish soap. Be sure to keep mixture out of pet's eyes. Follow with a washing of regular pet shampoo.

Antifreeze is deadly to pets. Promptly clean up any antifreeze spills, and keep pets away.

Be glad in the Lord.
– Psalm 32:11

My dog treats me like family. The cats treat me like staff.

– Ed Hector

Anybody who doesn't know what soap tastes like never washed a dog.

– Franklin P. Jones

23

To **clean your microwave** oven and remove odors, place an uncovered bowl of vinegar in the microwave and cook on "high" until it comes to a boil. Let the vinegar cool for a moment and then wipe the interior clean with a rag dipped in the vinegar.

To **deodorize a garbage disposal**, grind up half a lemon, orange or grapefruit in it. Never throw lemon rinds out, keep them in quarters in a plastic bag in your freezer. Throw a lemon rind quarter down the disposal whenever it starts to smell funny.

To **deodorize a microwave oven**, chop half a lemon into four pieces. Put them in a small bowl with one cup of water and a few whole cloves. Boil for five minutes.

*Create in me a clean heart, O God; and
renew a right spirit within me.*
– Psalm 51:10

*The other day I put instant coffee in my microwave
oven. . . . I almost went back in time.*

– Steven Wright

Club soda **removes stains** and cleans sinks.

Remove grime and grease from the oven door glass with baking soda on a damp cloth.

To **unclog a slow drain**, pour 1/2 cup baking soda in the drain. Then add one cup vinegar. Allow mixture to foam, then run hot water.

To **remove a stain** from the bottom of a glass vase or cruet, fill with water and drop in two Alka-Seltzer tablets.

Truly God is good to Israel, even to such as are of a clean heart.
– Psalm 73:1

Housework can't kill you, but why take a chance?

– Phyllis Diller

God is like Coke. . . . He's the real thing.

God is like General Electric. . . . He lights your path.

God is like Bayer. . . . He works wonders.

God is like Hallmark. . . . He cares enough to send the very best.

God is like Tide. . . . He gets the stains out that others leave behind.

God is like VO5. . . . He holds through all kinds of weather.

God is like Dial. . . . Aren't you glad you know Him ?

Don't you wish everybody did?

God is like Sears. . . . He has everything.

God is like Alka Seltzer. . . . Try Him: You'll like Him.

God is like Scotch Tape. . . . You can't see Him, but

you know He's there. [12]

All the ways of a man are clean in his own eyes;
but the LORD weigheth the spirits.
– Proverbs 16:2

I believe in getting into hot water; it keeps you clean.

– Gilbert Keith Chesterton

Simple Living

Tip

26

To **shine copper pots**, cut a lemon in half, put some salt on its surface, and rub it on the pot.

To **clean and polish the exterior of appliances**, use window cleaner.

Let everyone sweep in front of his own door and the whole world will be clean.

– Johann Wolfgang von Goethe

*The fear of the LORD is clean, enduring for ever: the judgments
of the LORD are true and righteous altogether.*

– Psalm 19:9

If dishes or plates are stained, soak overnight in a mixture of hot water and soda. Then rub with a vinegar-moistened cloth dipped in salt. This works very well with tea stains.

The Rose Bowl is the only bowl I've ever seen that I didn't have to clean.

– Erma Bombeck

And he made the vessels which were upon the table, his dishes, and his spoons, and his bowls, and his covers to cover withal, of pure gold.
– Exodus 37:16

Simple Living

Tip

28

10 Other Commandments To Live By

1. You shall not worry, for worry is the most unproductive of all human activities.

2. You shall not be fearful, for most of the things we fear never come to pass.

3. You shall not carry grudges, for they are the heaviest of all life's burdens.

4. You shall face each problem as it comes. You can only handle one at a time anyway.

5. You shall not take problems to bed with you, for they make very poor bedfellows.

6. You shall not borrow other people's problems. They can better care for them than you.

7. You shall not try to relive yesterday for good or ill, it is forever gone. Concentrate on what is happening in your life and be happy now!

8. You shall be a good listener, for only when you listen do you hear ideas different from your own.

9. You shall not become "bogged down" by frustration, for 90% of it is rooted in self-pity and will only interfere with positive action.

10. You shall count your blessings, never overlooking the small ones, for a lot of small blessings add up to a big one.[13]

The Ten Commandments aren't prefaced with "If you're in the mood."

– Laura Schlessinger

But lay up for yourselves treasures in heaven, where neither moth nor rust doth corrupt, and where thieves do not break through nor steal.

– Matthew 6:20

To **take the heat out of red onions**, after slicing them, put the slices into a bowl of cold water and soak for 10 minutes.

To **keep green chilis fresher** longer, remove the stems while storing them.

Use the water from cooked vegetables as **a stock for gravies** or soups.

To make **peeling tomatoes** easier, put tomatoes in a large bowl and cover with boiling water. Let stand for about 5 minutes, then peel.

> We remember the fish, which we did eat in Egypt freely; the cucumbers, and the melons, and the leeks, and the onions, and the garlick.
> – Numbers 11:5

> It's difficult to think anything but pleasant thoughts while eating a homegrown tomato.
> – Lewis Grizzard

30

Celery will last for weeks in the refrigerator when wrapped in aluminum foil or stored in water.

To **avoid crying while cutting onions**, after peeling, cut in half and soak in water for about ten minutes.

To **keep fruits and vegetables fresher** longer, wrap them in newspaper before refrigerating.

*And God said, Behold, I have given you every
herb bearing seed.*
– Genesis 1:29

*Vegetables are interesting but lack a sense of purpose
when unaccompanied by a good cut of meat.*

– Fran Lebowitz

Join a **supper club**. If you don't have time to cook each night, this is for you. One night per week, you cook identical dinners for each family in the co-op. On the other nights, your family eats a sit-down meal delivered — ready to heat and eat — by another. Find an interested family (or two or three), and lay down strict ground rules. Determine which foods are acceptable (is frozen lasagna OK?), the quantities and food groups to be included, and the delivery schedule. For best results, hook up with families who have similar tastes and schedules as your own.[14]

And Samuel said unto the cook, Bring the portion which I gave thee, of which I said unto thee, Set it by thee.
– 1 Samuel 9:23

We feel free when we escape — even if it be but from the frying pan to the fire.

– Eric Hoffer

To **avoid browning of apples** after cutting, apply a little lemon juice on the cut surface. The apples will stay and look fresh for a longer time.

To **keep apples fresh** for a long time, wrap each apple in tissue paper, and store them in a cool, dry place.

To **keep raisins fresher** longer, store in an airtight container in the refrigerator.

To **soften hardened raisins**, pour very hot water over them, drain immediately, then spread on paper towel to dry.

Keep me as the apple of the eye, hide me under the shadow of thy wings.
– Psalm 17:8

Anyone can count the seeds in an apple, but only God can count the number of apples in a seed.

– Robert H. Schuller

When **baking fruit pies**, cut the holes in the top of the crust with a thimble, then place the crust on the pie.

Now place the little cut outs back in place over the holes, which will have become larger.

Place a layer of marshmallows in the bottom of a **pumpkin pie**, then add the filling. They will make a nice topping because they will come to the top.

To keep all-purpose flour, semolina, and gram flour fresher longer and insect free, store them in airtight containers in the refrigerator.

The most convenient warm place in which batter or **dough can rise** is the inside of a switched-off oven with the light on.

How sweet are thy words unto my taste! yea,
sweeter than honey to my mouth!
– Psalm 119:103

Everyone is kneaded out of the same dough
but not baked in the same oven.

– Yiddish proverb

Simple Living

Tip

34

To **keep seeds and nuts** (both shelled and unshelled) fresher longer, store them in the freezer. Nuts in the shell crack more easily when frozen.

To **keep nuts from sticking** to the food processor when chopping, dust them beforehand with flour.

For **easy peeling of almonds**, soak in a cup of boiling water for ten minutes.

You'll get **more pop out of your popcorn** if you store it in the freezer and pop while still frozen.

The seed is the word of God.
– Luke 8:11

Of course life is bizarre, the more bizarre it gets, the more interesting it is. The only way to approach it is to make yourself some popcorn and enjoy the show.

– David Gerrold

To **core lettuce**, smack the core end of the head down hard on the counter top, then twist the core out.

Buy both ripe and not-so-ripe **fresh fruits and vegetables** so that the not-so-ripe items will last a few days longer and be ready for eating after you've finished the ripened ones.

When shopping for a **fresh head of lettuce**, turn it over and look at the base. If it shows any brownness, look for one with a greener base.

And having food and raiment "lettuce" be therewith content.
– 1 Timothy 6:8

You don't have to cook fancy or complicated master-pieces — just good food from fresh ingredients.

– Julia Child

To **keep milk from scorching**, rinse the pan with cold water before heating the milk.

To **make sour milk** out of sweet milk, add one tablespoon of vinegar or lemon juice to every cup of milk.

For ease of **chopping dried fruits**, freeze them first for one hour and then dip the knife into hot water before cutting them.

Freeze cooked grains. I freeze rice, quinoa, and millet in my small glass bowls. Frozen grains turn out fluffy, not mushy, when microwaved or cooked in a pan. Few people know that you can freeze grains.[15]

And I have said, I will bring you up out of the affliction of Egypt unto . . . a land flowing with milk and honey.
– Exodus 3:17

Avoid fruits and nuts. You are what you eat.

– Jim Davis in "Garfield"

Simple Living

Tip

37

Potatoes soaked in salt water for 20 minutes will bake more rapidly.

To **store peeled potatoes**, cover them with cold water and add a few drops of vinegar. They will last for three or four days in the refrigerator.

To avoid a brown edge to **day-old lettuce** used in a salad, tear the leaves instead of cutting them with a knife.

And the LORD God planted a garden eastward in Eden; and there he put the man whom he had formed.

– Genesis 2:8

Good thoughts bear good fruit, bad thoughts bear bad fruit — and man is his own gardener.

– James Lane Allen

38

Freeze ripe bananas whole, peeled, in plastic bags.

The best **storage place for dried herbs** and spices is in a cool, dark cupboard as heat is bad for them.

To **give apple slices a unique flavor** and prevent them from browning, place them in pineapple juice in the refrigerator.

And he shall be like a tree planted by the rivers of water, that bringeth forth his fruit in his season; his leaf also shall not wither; and whatsoever he doeth shall prosper.
– Psalm 1:3

An apple is an excellent thing — until you have tried a peach.

– George du Maurier

39

To lessen the mess when **making graham cracker crumbs**, put the graham crackers in a plastic bag and roll with a rolling pin.

Use herbs to **season salads** instead of salt.

Let a salad maker be a spendthrift for oil, a miser for vinegar, a statesman for salt, and a madman for mixing.
– Spanish proverb

To **prevent macaroni or spaghetti from sticking** or boiling over when cooking, add a few drops of salad oil to the water.

My beloved is gone down into his garden, to the beds of spices, to feed in the gardens, and to gather lilies.
– Song of Solomon 6:2

Simple Living
Tip

40

To **remove mud stains** from clothes, soak and wash them in water collected after boiling potatoes.

To **remove grass stains**, combine a few drops of household ammonia with one teaspoon of peroxide. Rub the stain with this mixture. Rinse with water as soon as the stain disappears.

Do not do what you would undo if caught.

–Leah Arendt

To **remove stains from a shirt collar**, mix baking soda and water into a paste. Scrub the paste gently on the stain using an old toothbrush before washing.

Then Jacob said unto his household, and to all that were with him, Put away the strange gods that are among you, and be clean, and change your garments.
– Genesis 35:2

As a moth gnaws a garment, so doth envy consume a man.

– Saint John Chrysostom

41

Did You Know That Fabric Softener Dryer Sheets:

Repel mosquitoes. Tie a sheet through a belt loop when outdoors during mosquito season.

Eliminate static electricity from your television or computer screen. Wipe your television screen with a used sheet to keep dust from resettling.

Dissolve soap scum from shower doors. Clean with a used sheet.

Freshen the air in your home. Place an individual sheet in a drawer or hang one in the closet.

Prevent thread from tangling. Run a threaded needle through a sheet to eliminate the static cling on the thread before sewing.

Eliminate static cling from hose. Rub a damp, used sheet over the hose.

Prevent musty suitcases. Place an individual sheet inside empty luggage before storing.

Freshen the air in your car. Place a sheet under the front seat.

Clean baked-on food from a cooking pan. Put a sheet in the pan, fill with water, let sit overnight, and sponge clean. The antistatic agents apparently weaken the bond between the food and the pan while the fabric softening agents soften the baked-on food.

Eliminate odors in wastebaskets. Place a sheet at the bottom of the wastebasket.

Collect cat hair. Rubbing the area with a sheet will magnetically attract all the loose hairs.

Eliminate static electricity from Venetian blinds. Wipe the blinds with a sheet to prevent dust from resettling.

Deodorize shoes or sneakers. Place a sheet in your shoes or sneakers overnight so they'll smell great in the morning.

Prevent hair static. Rub a sheet on hairbrushes to prevent static cling or gently rub on your hair to eliminate static.

Chase ants away. Lay a sheet near them.

Repel mice. Spread the sheets around foundation areas, or in trailers or cars that are sitting and it keeps mice from entering your vehicle.

Take the odor out of books and photo albums that don't get opened too often.

Freshen as you vacuum. Put a sheet in vacuum cleaner.

Wipe up sawdust from drilling or sand papering. A used sheet will collect sawdust like a tack cloth.

Keep the bees away. Golfers, put a sheet in your back pocket.

Keep sleeping bags and tents smelling fresh. Put a sheet in them before folding and storing them.

Note: You will probably want to use an unscented sheet.

It is one of the severest tests of friendship to tell your friend his faults. So to love a man that you cannot bear to see a stain upon him, and to speak painful truth through loving words, that is friendship.

– Henry Ward Beecher

42

To **remove ball-point pen ink marks,** use rubbing alcohol.

To **prevent garments from discoloring**, soak the garments for ten minutes in salt water prior to initial washing. An alternative is to add a few drops of vinegar to the wash cycle.

Oil stain may be removed by rubbing the area with a piece of lime dipped in salt.

Remove **ink stain** from a cloth by applying toothpaste on both sides of the cloth. When the toothpaste dries out, wash the cloth.

Bloodstains in clothing should be removed as soon as possible. Use cold water and wash out the stain. Hot water will set the blood and it will be difficult or impossible to get out.

And the LORD said unto Moses, Go unto the people, and sanctify them to day and to morrow, and let them wash their clothes.
– Exodus 19:10

43

Your **washing machine should be cleaned** every six months. Fill it with very hot to boiling water, add two gallons of vinegar and let it agitate for eight to ten minutes. Turn the machine off and let it stand overnight. In the morning, turn machine on and let it run through a complete cycle.

For she said, If I may touch but his clothes, I shall be whole.
– Mark 5:28

To **remove perspiration stains** from clothing, add water to four tablespoons of baking soda, to make a thick paste. Rub into the stained area and let sit for an hour. Wash as usual.

Always **hang your silk clothes** on plastic or padded hangers. Metal or wooden hangers leave small creases or imprints in the garments.

> *Positive reinforcement is hugging your husband when he does a load of laundry. Negative reinforcement is telling him he used too much detergent.*
>
> – Dr. Joyce Brothers

To **keep shower doors shiny and clear**, use a soft cloth moistened with baby oil. It prevents scum build-up from dirt and soap. And hard water spots won't appear for several months. Or prevent soap scum from accumulating on shower doors by applying a light coat of lemon oil. The oil will also keep doors shiny and the bathroom smelling fresher.

Remove soap scum quickly and easily with a laundry stain treatment such as Spray 'n' Wash. Spray on and wipe off.

And that ye may put difference between holy and unholy, and between unclean and clean.
– Leviticus 10:10

Scrubbing floors and emptying bedpans has as much dignity as the presidency.
– Richard M. Nixon

45

Use newspaper instead of paper towels to **clean mirrors** or glass. You'll save money on the cost of paper towels, and the printer's ink will leave a protective shiny coat on the glass.

To **make glass and mirrors sparkle**, dissolve one tablespoon of cornstarch in a quart of water to use as the cleaning agent.

To **make the chrome really shine** on your faucets use rubbing alcohol.[16]

Wash, and be clean.
 – 2 Kings 5:13

The best mirror is an old friend.

– George Herbert

Law of window cleaning: It's on the other side.

– Anonymous

46

Keep a **bar of soap** on a sponge to prevent it from becoming soggy. You can use the soapy sponge to clean the basin and the tap.

Keep a bucket or basket of basic supplies under each sink so you don't have to hunt for cleaning supplies. It's much easier to clean a bathroom in a hurry if the supplies are all ready, rather than going to different parts of the house to collect the necessary items.

Try make-up baskets. I have one ten-inch round basket for make-up (brushes, shadows, cover-up, etc) and a small square basket for lipsticks. Both baskets sit on a white-wire step shelf under my bathroom sink. My scale fits neatly under the shelf.[17]

And ye shall wash your clothes on the seventh day,
and ye shall be clean.
– Numbers 31:24

The reason there are so few female politicians is that
it is too much trouble to put makeup on two faces.

– Maureen Murphy

47

Avoid reaching over the stove for anything while cooking. Store frequently needed items in other areas of the kitchen.

Shield yourself from steam when uncovering food especially microwave servings. Steam can cause serious burns.

Always turn pot handles toward the back of the stove so no one accidentally bumps into them and knocks a pot over.

Clean grease build-up from the stove, oven, and exhaust fan regularly. Cooking grease and oil ignite easily and burn rapidly.

And though I bestow all my goods to feed the poor, and though I give my body to be burned, and have not charity, it profiteth me nothing.
– 1 Corinthians 13:3

Tears are the safety valve of the heart when too much pressure is laid on it.

– Albert Smith

Simple Living

Tip

48

Always **wash your hands** in hot, soapy water, scrubbing for 10-15 seconds before and after handling raw meat, poultry, seafood, or eggs.

Wash fresh fruits and vegetables thoroughly.

Man did eat angels' food: he sent them meat to the full.
– Psalm 78:25

Always make sure your **knives are kept** clean and sharpened. A dull knife is more dangerous than a sharp one, because it will slip more easily. Never cut toward you or down into your hand.

> My wife, she can't cook at all. When we go on a picnic, I bring Tums for the ants.
>
> – Rodney Dangerfield

Simple Living
Tip

49

Use fluorescent bulbs when possible. A 40-watt fluorescent bulb gives twice the light of a 100-watt incandescent and uses less electricity.

To avoid retying children's shoelaces many times in a day, wipe them with a wet cloth before you tie them the first time. They will stay tied all day.

Put a bucket under your gutter spout to catch rainwater. Use it to water houseplants and also for washing hair. Both will be healthier.

In the spring, **scatter pieces of yarn** around the shrubs for the birds to use in building nests.

But even the very hairs of your head are all numbered. Fear not therefore: ye are of more value than many sparrows.

– Luke 12:7

50

To **make candles burn longer** and not drip, chill them for 24 hours in the refrigerator before using.

To **remove gum from hair**, rub peanut butter in the hair, then wash.

Avoid opening the oven door. While cooking or baking something in the oven, every time you open the oven door to check something, the temperature drops about 25 degrees.

To get rid of a lingering **onion smell** on your hands, trying rinsing with cold water, rubbing with salt, and then rewashing. Another remedy is to rub hands with half of a potato.

*I wash myself with snow water, and make my
hands never so clean.*
– Job 9:30

There is no odor so bad as that which arises from goodness tainted.

– Henry David Thoreau

Simple Living
Tip

51

In October, **caladiums** can be lifted, dried, and stored for later spring planting. **Banana plants** can be wrapped or moved to a protected area to keep above freezing for the winter.[18]

To create a garden is to search for a better world. In our effort to improve on nature, we are guided by a vision of paradise. Whether the result is a horticultural masterpiece or only a modest vegetable patch, it is based on the expectation of a glorious future. This hope for the future is at the heart of all gardening.

– Marina Schinz

. . . all the goodliness thereof is as the flower of the field.

– Isaiah 40:6

52

If you've been pampering last year's **poinsettias**, October is the time to complete the task. Poinsettias need about 14 hours of uninterrupted darkness per day beginning October first in order to bloom in full color for the Christmas season.

At most garden centers, variety and selection of **shade trees** is at an all-time high. Fall is the time for planting.

For areas plagued by fire ants, late spring and early fall are the best times to treat individual mounds. Each fall rain shower seems to be followed by mounds popping up everywhere. Chemicals considered to be bait are more effective than contact insecticides because the worker ants will transport chemical bait particles to the queen, destroying the colony.[19]

They shall come and sing aloud on the height of Zion, and they shall be radiant over the goodness of the LORD, over the grain, the wine, and the oil, and over the young of the flock and the herd; their life shall be like a watered garden, and they shall languish no more.
— Jeremiah 31:12

For a good **house plant fertilizer** and insecticide, dispose of coffee and tea grounds and crushed egg shells in the house plant's soil.

Destroy weeds in walkways by spreading a generous amount of salt there. Apply early in the growing season, and reapply as necessary.

To clean a barbecue grill rack, lay it on the lawn overnight. The dew will combine with the enzymes in the grass to loosen any burned-on grease. Try it with

The grass withereth, the flower fadeth: but the word of our God shall stand for ever.
– Isaiah 40:8

In my garden there is a large place for sentiment. My garden of flowers is also my garden of thoughts and dreams. The thoughts grow as freely as the flowers, and the dreams are as beautiful.

– Abram L. Urban

54

God's Garden

Plant three rows of squash:

1. Squash gossip.

2. Squash criticism.

3. Squash indifference.

Plant seven rows of peas:

1. Prayer

2. Promptness

3. Perseverance

4. Politeness

5. Preparedness

6. Purity

7. Patience

Plant seven heads of lettuce:

1. Let us be unselfish and loyal.

2. Let us be faithful to duty.

3. Let us search the scriptures.

4. Let us not be weary in well doing.

5. Let us be obedient in all things.

6. Let us be truthful.

7. Let us love one another.

No garden is complete without turnips:

1. Turn up for church.

2. Turn up for meetings, in prayer, and Bible study.

3. Turn up with a smile, even when things are difficult.

4. Turn up with determination to do your best in God's service for Jesus Christ (2 Peter 3:18). And may you reap rich results.

Make sure your garden gets **plenty of exposure** to the SON!

Whatsoever a man soweth, that shall he also reap.
– Galatians 6:7

There's nothing like listening to a shower and thinking how it is soaking in around your green beans.

– Marcelene Cox

55

Have your child teach you something.

Be attentive. This can range from a hilarious description from a three year old to an astonishing learning experience with a ten year old. Your teenager can teach you some new slang words, or about the latest rock or new age band, maybe even a dance step. Be prepared to learn. Your kids know a lot more than you think they do. Next time they mention something they are really excited about, ask them to teach you a little more. And pay attention![20]

> *If you want your children to keep their feet on the ground, put some responsibility on their shoulders.*
>
> – Abigail Van Buren

Use some of your errand and shopping time as a special time together. One mother reports that her four year old considers grocery shopping their special time together. Yes, this mother does have to allow extra time to get the shopping done, but the payback is well worth it. Her son gets to pick out his cereal for the week, assist in putting some of the groceries in the cart, and even push the cart when the store is not crowded.[21]

The LORD shall increase you more and more, you and your children.
– Psalm 115:14

Never lend your car to anyone to whom you have given birth.

– Erma Bombeck

57

Use everyday chores as a special time together with your child. Have your child help you with the laundry, or getting dinner ready. This is not a time to try to make your child perform the chore perfectly; it's a time to chat and giggle while you work together. Let your child do whatever part they can handle and enjoy. For example, your child may be too young to wash the dishes, but just old enough to rinse the silverware and the non-breakable dishes and put them in the drainer. Be creative![22]

> *The best inheritance a parent can give to his children is a few minutes of his time each day.*
>
> – M. Grundler

58

Combine exercise time with quality time. Ask your child to ride their bike around the block while you jog. Ask them to walk with you, or for the little ones, push them in a stroller. A father reports that his child doesn't even mind getting up early to be able to exercise with Daddy.[23]

For this child I prayed; and the LORD hath given me my petition which I asked of him: Therefore also I have lent him to the LORD; as long as he liveth he shall be lent to the LORD.

– 1 Samuel 1:27-28

Simple Living

Tip

59

- **Pray for your husband's spiritual condition;** pray that God would help him see the need to pray with you.

- Ask the Lord to show you ways to **build confidence** in your partner.

- **Pray for yourself.** Is there something in your life that could be hindering spiritual intimacy between you and your husband?

- **Encourage your husband.** Acknowledge, in a positive way, the small steps he might take in spiritual matters. Celebrate any progress made.

- **Don't give up.** Being patient can be challenging, especially in this microwaved, results-now oriented world; however, Paul reminds us that love is patient. It never seeks its own way (1 Corinthians 13).[24]

And the LORD God said, It is not good that the man should be alone; I will make him an help meet for him.
– Genesis 2:18

An archaeologist is the best husband any woman can have; the older she gets, the more interested he is in her.
– Agatha Christie

60

Make It Great with Your Mate!

End an argument fast. Seal it with a kiss.

Make each day special in some way.

When you quarrel, don't call home to Mother.

Enjoy laughter with your husband.

Don't make him your entire life; that drains a marriage.

Never laugh at your husband's dreams.

Teach your husband the art of cuddling.

Hold hands often.

Plan outings for just the two of you.

Never put him down in front of someone.

Learn to keep a private talk private.

Be a patient listener. What he has to say is important, too.

Plan time with other couples your age.

Be happy by making the most of what you have.

Never let a day go by without saying, "I love you."

Keep yourself looking pretty.

Use his favorite perfume.

Hold hands during a movie.

Marriage is work, but work can bring extreme pleasure.

Always keep your bedroom fresh, neat, and inviting.[25]

A successful marriage is not a gift; it is an achievement.

– Ann Landers

Marriage is honourable in all.
– Hebrews 13:4

Simple Living

Tip

61

For attractive lips, speak words of kindness.

For lovely eyes, seek out the good in people.

For a slim figure, share your food with the hungry.

For beautiful hair, let a child run his/her fingers through it once a day.

For poise, walk with the knowledge that you never walk alone.

People, even more than things, have to be restored, renewed, revived, reclaimed, and redeemed; never throw out anyone.

Remember, if you ever need a helping hand, you will find one at the end of each of your arms.

As you grow older, you will discover that you have two hands; one for helping yourself, and the other for helping others.[26]

Who can say, I have made my heart clean, I am pure from my sin?
– Proverbs 20:9

Do you have **puffy, tired eyes?** Lay back, relax and place cold tea bags over your tired eyes. Leave on for 5 or 10 minutes. You will be amazed at how much better you will look and feel.

The light of the body is the eye.

– Jesus Christ

. . . to give unto them beauty for ashes, the oil of joy for mourning, the garment of praise for the spirit of heaviness; that they might be called trees of righteousness, the planting of the LORD, that he might be glorified.

– Isaiah 61:3

63

Eat Right

The Japanese eat very little fat and suffer fewer heart attacks than the British or Americans. The French eat a lot of fat and also suffer fewer heart attacks than the British or Americans.

The Japanese drink very little red wine and suffer fewer heart attacks than the British or Americans. The Italians drink excessive amounts of red wine and also suffer fewer heart attacks than the British or Americans.

The Germans drink a lot of beers and eat lots of sausages and fats and suffer fewer heart attacks than the British or Americans.

Conclusion: Eat and drink what you like. Apparently, speaking English is what kills you.

For every creature of God is good, and nothing to be refused, if it be received with thanksgiving.
– 1 Timothy 4:4

I eat right. I'm in shape. Round is a shape, isn't it?
– Anonymous

64

Don't Deceive Yourself

While waiting for my first appointment in the reception room of a new dentist, I noticed his certificate, which bore his full name.

Suddenly, I remembered that a handsome boy with the same name had been in my high school class some 40 years ago. Upon seeing him, however, I quickly discarded any such thought. This balding, gray-haired man with the deeply lined face was too old to have been my classmate. After he had examined my teeth, I asked him if he had attended the local high school.

"Yes," he replied.

"When did you graduate?" I asked.

He answered, "In 1957."

"Why, you were in my class!" I exclaimed.

He looked at me closely and then asked, "What did you teach?"

Let no man [or woman!] deceive himself.
– 1 Cor. 3:18

65

Find Some Peace of Mind

Duke University did a study on "peace of mind." Factors found to contribute greatly to emotional and mental stability are:

1. The absence of suspicion and resentment. Nursing a grudge was a major factor in unhappiness.

2. Not living in the past. An unwholesome preoccupation with old mistakes and failures leads to depression.

3. Not wasting time and energy fighting conditions you cannot change. Cooperate with life, instead of trying to run away from it.

4. Forcing yourself to stay involved with the living world. Resist the temptation to withdraw and become reclusive during periods of emotional stress.

5. Refusing to indulge in self-pity when life hands you a raw deal. Accept the fact that nobody gets through life without some sorrow and misfortune. Cultivate the old-fashioned virtues — love, humor, compassion and loyalty.

6. Not expecting too much of yourself. When there is too wide a gap between self-expectation and your

ability to meet the goals you have set, feelings of inadequacy are inevitable.

7. Finding something bigger than yourself to believe in. Self-centered, egotistical people score lowest in any test for measuring happiness.[27]

Of course these principles lead to peace of mind! The Bible has expounded these truths for many years, even if the researchers at Duke thought they had come up with something new. Here are verses reflecting the gist of each point above.

Suspicion and Resentment

Forbearing one another, and forgiving one another, if any man have a quarrel against any: even as Christ forgave you, so also do ye (Colossians 3:13).

Not Living in the Past

This one thing I do, forgetting those things which are behind, and reaching forth unto those things which are before (Philippians 3:13).

Fighting Conditions You Cannot Change

Not that I speak in respect of want: for I have learned, in whatsoever state I am, therewith to be content (Philippians 4:11).

Staying Involved with the World

And he said unto them, Go ye into all the world, and preach the gospel to every creature (Mark 16:15).

Refusing to Indulge in Self Pity

Take, my brethren, the prophets, who have spoken in the name of the Lord, for an example of suffering affliction, and of patience. Behold, we count them happy which endure (James 5:10-11).

Not Expecting Too Much of Yourself

For I say, through the grace given unto me, to every man that is among you, not to think of himself more highly than he ought to think; but to think soberly, according as God hath dealt to every man the measure of faith (Romans 12:3).

Finding Something Bigger Than Yourself To Believe In

Let not your heart be troubled: ye believe in God, believe also in me (John 14:1).

Watch and pray, that ye enter not into temptation:
the spirit indeed is willing, but the flesh is weak.
– Matthew 26:41

Watch your thoughts; they become words.
Watch your words; they become actions.
Watch your actions; they become habits.
Watch your habits; they become character.
Watch your character; it becomes your destiny.

– Frank Outlaw

66

Use a Special Makeup for Your Complexion

A dear old lady was asked what she used to make her complexion so beautiful and her whole being so bright and attractive. She answered:

I use for my lips truth;

I use for my voice kindness;

I use for my ears compassion;

I use for my hands charity;

I use for my figure uprightness;

I use for my heart love;

I use for anyone who doesn't like me prayer.

And above all these things put on charity, which is the bond of perfectness. And let the peace of God rule in your hearts, to the which also ye are called in one body; and be ye thankful. Let the word of Christ dwell in you richly in all wisdom; teaching and admonishing one another in psalms and hymns and spiritual songs, singing with grace in your hearts to the Lord. And whatsoever ye do in word or deed, do all in the name of the Lord Jesus, giving thanks to God and the Father by him.
– Colossians 3:14-17

References

[1] Adapted from *The Circle of Simplicity* by Cecile Andrews.

[2] Ramona Creel, professional organizer and founder of OnlineOrganizing.com.

[3] Author Unknown; Valerie Wells's The Master's Touch website.

[4] *Homelife* magazine.

[5] Author Unknown; Valerie Wells's The Master's Touch website.

[6] Ramona Creel, professional organizer and founder of OnlineOrganizing.com.

[7] *Woman's World* magazine.

[8] Ramona Creel, professional organizer and founder of OnlineOrganizing.com.

[9] *Simple Living* magazine.

[10] Ramona Creel, professional organizer and founder of OnlineOrganizing.com.

[11] Author Unknown; Valerie Wells's The Masters Touch website.

[12] Author Unknown; Valerie Wells's The Master's Touch website.

[13] Author Unknown; Valerie Wells's The Master's Touch website.

[14] *Homelife* magazine.

[15] *Simple Living* magazine.

[16] *Simple Living* magazine.

[17] *Simple Living* magazine.

[18] *Homelife* magazine.

[19] *Homelife* magazine.

[20] Simple Life Corporation.

[21] Simple Life Corporation.

[22] Simple Life Corporation.

[23] Simple Life Corporation.

[24] *Homelife* magazine.

[25] Clara Hinton, *Tender Thoughts for Couples.*

[26] Sam Levinson.

[27] Sermon Illustrations.

Simple Living

Photo Credits